YOU CHOOSE
BOOKS

The SINKING of the LUSITANIA

An Interactive History Adventure

by Steven Otfinoski

Consultant:
Doran Cart, Senior Curator
National World War I Museum
Kansas City, Missouri

CAPSTONE PRESS
a capstone imprint

You Choose Books are published by Capstone Press,
1710 Roe Crest Drive, North Mankato, Minnesota 56003
www.capstonepub.com

Library of Congress Cataloging-in-Publication Data
The sinking of the Lusitania : an interactive history adventure/by Steven Otfinoski.
    pages cm. – (You choose books. you choose: history.)
  Includes bibliographical references and index.
  Summary: "Describes the sinking of the Lusitania. Readers' choices reveal various
historical details"— Provided by publisher.
  ISBN 978-1-4765-4186-0 (library binding)
  ISBN 978-1-4765-5217-0 (paperback)
  ISBN 978-1-4765-6063-2 (eBook PDF)
1. Lusitania (Steamship)—Juvenile literature. 2. World War, 1914–1918—Naval
operations—Submarine—Juvenile literature. I. Title.
  D592.L8O86 2014
  940.4'514—dc23   2013034940

Editorial Credits
Brenda Haugen, editor; Bobbie Nuytten, designer; Wanda Winch, media researcher;
Danielle Ceminsky, production specialist

Printed in the United States of America in North Mankato, Minnesota.
052015   008938R

TABLE OF CONTENTS

About Your Adventure

YOU live in a world at war. It's 1915, and World War I erupted a year earlier. The United States has remained neutral, but an event is about to take place that will help bring the U.S. into the war. How will this event affect you?

In this book you'll explore how the choices people made meant the difference between life and death. The events you'll experience really happened.

Chapter One sets the scene. Then you choose which path to read. Follow the directions at the bottom of each page. The choices you make will change your outcome. After you finish one path, go back and read the others for new perspectives and more adventures.

YOU CHOOSE the path
you take through history.

The *Lusitania* arrives for
the first time in New York
September 13, 1907.

TRAVEL IN A DANGEROUS TIME

While Europe was at war in 1915, life in the United States went on peacefully. People enjoyed themselves. One source of pleasure, for those who could afford it, was crossing the Atlantic Ocean on a luxury liner. Cunard, a ship company in England, built and sailed some of the greatest of the passenger ships. The *Lusitania*, finished in 1907, was one of the biggest and most luxurious of the ships. It was 785 feet long, had eight decks, and could hold 3,000 passengers and crewmembers. Although other ships, such as *Titanic*, were bigger, no passenger ship was faster. The *Lusitania's* four turbine engines propelled the ship to an average speed of about 25 knots.

Turn the page.

United States

New York

Atlantic Ocean

In August 1914, the month after the war broke out, there were only three Cunard passenger ships still operating. The *Lusitania* was one of them.

But the *Lusitania* carried more than passengers. The cost of building the ships was so high that Cunard sought financial aid from the British. In exchange for money to build ships, Cunard carried supplies for the government. When war with Germany broke out, the *Lusitania* regularly carried wartime supplies from the U.S. to England.

Irish Sea

IRELAND

Queenstown

Liverpool

London

ENGLAND

The *Lusitania* was traveling from New York to Liverpool.

German officials knew some commercial liners were carrying secret shipments. They were also angry at England for the naval blockade it had set up in 1914. The British Grand Fleet prevented German ships from leaving their home waters. It also prevented foreign ships carrying supplies, including food, from reaching Germany.

Turn the page.

The Germans announced they were establishing a war zone in the waters surrounding the British Isles in February 1915. German submarines, called U-boats, traveled underwater and could get through the British blockade to reach the area. Germany vowed to attack any merchant ships in these waters.

Angered by the announcement, U.S. President Woodrow Wilson told Germany it would be accountable for any American lives or property lost in such attacks.

A German submarine patrols during World War I.

The *Lusitania* prepared to sail from New York Harbor on its 202nd Atlantic crossing on May 1, 1915. Aboard were 702 crewmembers and 1,257 passengers, including 129 children. While most of the passengers were British, there were more than 150 Americans onboard. You are aboard the *Lusitania* on what will be its last voyage.

➤ To be an American boy traveling to England with his family in second class, turn to page **13**.

➤ To be a young British woman on her honeymoon with her husband in first class, turn to page **41**.

➤ To be an American sailor hired in New York to serve on the Lusitania, turn to page **73**.

Passengers relax on the deck of the *Lusitania*.

BOY ON BOARD

It is May 1, 1915. *Lusitania* is about to sail
from New York, and you and your family are
onboard. You are one lucky 12-year-old! As the
ship sets sail, you decide to go exploring. There
are eight decks, and you can explore most of
them. You invite your younger sister, Miriam, to
join you, but she'd rather stay with your mother.
She's such a baby.

You race through a lounge area and
find yourself in a fancy room with marble
mantelpieces. Suddenly a man's voice speaks
sharply. "What are doing in here, boy?" You turn
to see a man in a white uniform glaring at you.
"This room is for gentlemen, not children," the
man says to you.

Turn the page.

A tall, handsome man sitting nearby speaks up. "It's all right, Jameson. The boy means no harm."

The man in the uniform changes his tone instantly. "Very well, Mr. Vanderbilt," he says, and moves away.

Alfred Vanderbilt rises from his chair and looks you over. "Is this your first time on the *Lusitania*, lad?" he asks you.

"First time on any ship, sir," you reply.

Vanderbilt smiles. "I've made this trip across the sea so many times that it means nothing to me. But to you it must be a great adventure."

"Yes, it is, sir," you tell him. You like this Mr. Vanderbilt.

He walks with you out on deck and asks about your family. Then he says he hopes to see you again and strolls down the deck. Later you tell your parents about your meeting with the friendly man.

"Alfred Vanderbilt?" your father gasps. "He's from one of the richest families in America."

You don't see Vanderbilt again, but you meet a number of children your own age and have lots of adventures.

It is now May 7, and your trip across the Atlantic is nearly at an end. You have just finished eating lunch with your family when there is a loud noise above deck. "What happened?" your father asks a crewmember when you go on deck.

Turn the page.

"We've been hit by a German torpedo, sir. Best to get your wife and children into a lifeboat. Just in case."

On the port side of the ship, men are helping people into lifeboats and then lowering the boats to the water. "Are you sure this is necessary, John?" your mother asks, looking anxiously at your father.

Women and children are loaded into a lifeboat.

"The man said it's a safety precaution," your father says. "The ship will be fine. But you must go with the children for now."

Your mother gathers you and Miriam and gets in line for the next lifeboat. If it's just a precaution, you would rather stay with your father. You don't want to leave him alone. You are almost to the front of the line and about to get into the lifeboat. You'd better make up your mind.

➻ To go with your mother in the lifeboat, turn to page **18**.

➻ To stay with your father, turn to page **20**.

You decide your mother needs you more than your father right now. You get into the lifeboat alongside your mother and Miriam. Your mother helps Miriam get into her life jacket. You put on your own. The men start to lower the lifeboat down to the water many feet below.

But something's wrong. The lifeboat's weight limit was surpassed when you climbed aboard. The boat jerks back and forth, hitting the side of the ship. As the hole made by the torpedo fills with water, the ship starts to sink and list to one side. The lifeboat is at the wrong angle and keeps bumping against the ship. Suddenly there is a crashing sound, and the lifeboat breaks apart. The next thing you know, you are falling.

You hit the water with a loud splash. You shiver from the cold and wave your arms about. There are people splashing all around you.

You don't see your mother, but suddenly you hear a familiar cry. It's Miriam. She is a dozen feet or more away in the water. "Help!" she cries.

Nearby you see a lifeboat. It is drawing close to you. An old man stands in the prow of the boat. He extends a hand to you. "Come on, son," he says, "Get on board."

"But my sister is over there," you tell him. "She can't swim."

"We'll get to her in a minute," says the man. "Take my hand."

Do you allow yourself to be rescued? Or is getting to your sister more important?

➻ To swim to your sister, turn to page **22**.
➻ To get into the lifeboat, turn to page **32**.

You step out of line, much to your mother's distress, and you rush to your father's side. "You've got to stay with your mother and sister," your father insists.

"I won't leave you here alone," you say. Your father sighs and tells your mother he will put you on the next lifeboat.

Their lifeboat is lowered, and you and your dad watch your mother and sister land safely on the swirling waters below.

The crew has stopped lowering any more lifeboats from the port side, saying it's too dangerous. "Let's go starboard and see if they are lowering lifeboats there," says your father.

They are, and one boat has already started its descent from the side of the ship. There are several open spaces in the lifeboat. Your father pulls you to the edge of the ship.

"You can jump and make it into the boat," he says.

The boat is about a dozen feet below. If you jump and miss, it's 50 feet to the water and almost certain death.

"You can make it," your father whispers in your ear.

Can you? Would it be wiser and safer to stay aboard with him?

➤ To stay with your father, turn to page 24.

➤ To jump for the lifeboat, turn to page 31.

You go to your sister. You're a good swimmer and make it to her side in seconds. She screams and grabs you. With one arm around her waist, you slice through the water with your other arm. You reach the side of the lifeboat, and the old man peers at you.

"Don't let them on," cries a large woman in the boat. "We'll capsize!"

Others shout their agreement. The old man hesitates to take your hand.

You have two options. You can try to convince the people to take your sister, who won't take up much room. Or you can force your way on board for both of you.

✦ To get your sister aboard, turn to page **33**.

✦ To force your way on, turn to page **34**.

The *Lusitania* sank within sight of the Irish coast.

Blarney Castle

Shandon

River Lee

CORK

Railway

Blackrock

Railway

QUEENSTOWN

Carrigaline

Innishannon

BANDON

KINSALE

OLD HEAD of KINSALE

KINSALE HARBOUR, where several boat loads of survivors were towed by a Greek steamer

Power Head

All the vessels leaving QUEENSTOWN & hastening to the wreck 30 miles away reaching the scene 1 to 2 hours after the Lusitania had sunk. H.M.S.Stormock brought back 160 survivors, the Trawlers Bock and Indian Empire about 200, the Tug "Flying Fish" about 100 and 3 Torpedo Boats 45 survivors; many were brought in by Fishing vessels.

The LUSITANIA sinking on her starboard side in about 300 feet of water, and 8 miles South by West of the Old Head of Kinsale.

Only two of the BOATS on this, the port side could be launched owing to the list, but about 20 were got off from the other side.

Where the second torpedo was reported to have penetrated

Where the first torpedo penetrated the Engine Room

TRACK of the TORPEDO

Position of the PIRATE SUBMARINE about 200 yards from the LUSITANIA, from which its cowardly GERMAN Crew were able to MURDER over 1400 innocent and defenceless people, without fear of retaliation

G.F. MORRELL

23

Turn the page.

"It's too far," you tell your father. "I'll never make it."

"All right," he says, drawing you closer to him. "But we've got to get you a life jacket." He tries to get a jacket from one of the crew rushing by, but the man says they are out of them.

"Stay here and don't move," your father finally says to you. "I'm going below deck to find life jackets. I'll be back as soon as I can."

You want to go with him, but he says he'll make better time without you. Minutes pass, and there is no sign of your father.

Suddenly you hear a familiar voice, saying, "What are you doing here alone?" It's Mr. Vanderbilt. He is dressed in a suit and wears a life jacket.

"I'm waiting for my father," you say. "But I don't know where he is."

"How long have you been waiting?" he asks.

You try to hold back the tears, but it's hopeless. "A long time," you say, sobbing.

"Don't cry," Vanderbilt says, pulling a handkerchief from his pocket and wiping your eyes with it. "Here, I have something for you."

He takes off his life jacket and puts it on you. Just then a young woman holding a baby in her arms runs up to the two of you.

"Please, sir," she cries to Vanderbilt. "Can you help us?"

Vanderbilt tries to comfort her, but she is distraught. You realize that she doesn't have a life jacket.

→ To give the woman your life jacket, turn to page **26**.

→ To keep the life jacket, turn to page **30**.

You know you couldn't live with yourself if you didn't give your life jacket to the woman. "Here," you say, removing the jacket. "You'll be safer with this."

Vanderbilt stares at you and then helps the woman put on the life jacket.

"Now go find a lifeboat that's not full and get into it," he tells her. "And hold on tight to that child."

The woman quickly makes her way down the deck. Vanderbilt squeezes your shoulder.

"That was a courageous thing you did, my boy," he says. "I know your father would be proud of you right now."

Your father. For a moment you'd forgotten about him. "Can you help me find him, Mr. Vanderbilt?" you ask.

You can feel the deck shifting under your feet. "I don't know, son," he says. "There isn't much time left."

You suddenly see your father approaching. He is holding two life jackets in his hands. "Quick, get the jackets on," says Vanderbilt. "There isn't much time."

As your father helps you with your life jacket, he looks at Vanderbilt. "Excuse me, sir," he says, "but where is your life jacket?"

"I'll be fine," he says. "But you and your son need to move fast if you're going to get into a lifeboat."

"A crewmember just told me that there are no more lifeboats being lowered," your father says. "Then you should go to the side of the ship and jump for it," says Vanderbilt.

Turn the page.

"Aren't you coming with us?" you ask Mr. Vanderbilt.

"No, son," Vanderbilt replies. "I don't want to get my suit wet. And anyway, I can't swim. Now go."

Your father thanks him, and you rush to the railing.

"Are you ready to jump?" your father asks. He looks afraid.

You don't know if you can do it. Maybe you should stay on board and take your chances with Mr. Vanderbilt. He doesn't seem so afraid.

➤ To jump, go to page **29**.

➤ To stay on the ship, turn to page **36**.

"We've got to do it, son," your father says.

He holds your hand and counts to three. Together you leap into the water. You hold your breath as you sink and then, still holding your father's hand, bob up to the surface.

All around you people are flailing their arms. It's a sea of bodies. "We've got to swim as far from the ship as we can," your father says.

You swim side by side. You're sure your father could swim faster, but he slows down for you. Soon your arms ache and you're so tired you can hardly breathe.

Your father sees your condition and stops. "Here," he says pointing. "Grab on to that piece of driftwood."

Turn to page 37.

You keep the life jacket, but you feel a sense of shame in doing so. You move away from Mr. Vanderbilt and the woman. He is busy trying to calm her down and doesn't see you leave.

"Where did you get the life jacket?" a man with wild eyes snarls at you. He grabs you roughly. You try to break away, but the man pulls at the straps of your life jacket. "Don't!" you cry. "You'll rip it!"

You lose your footing and fall. The man goes down too. Together you roll to the railing and tumble over the side. You try to swim, but the man is tightly holding you. He won't let go. Together you sink down, down, down into the depths of the ocean.

THE END

To follow another path, turn to page 11.
To read the conclusion, turn to page 101.

You focus on the boat swaying below and jump. You land in the boat with a thud. You look up and see your father above looking down and waving at you. You wave back. Later, when rescue boats arrive from shore, you will be reunited with your mother and sister on land. But you will never see your dear father again. Like hundreds of other people, he went down with the *Lusitania*.

People cling to lifeboats and driftwood as the *Lusitania* sinks.

THE END

To follow another path, turn to page 11.
To read the conclusion, turn to page 101.

You take the man's hand, and he pulls you into the lifeboat. You are happy to see there is room for your sister. But when the people row over to where you last saw your sister in the water, she is no longer there. You frantically scan the water. There are so many people in the water it's hard to tell who is who.

"You've got to look for her!" you say to the old man.

He shakes his head. "Sorry, son," he says. "We've got to get away from the ship before it goes down and sucks us under with it."

You begin to cry. If you had not been so quick to save yourself, you might have been able to save your sister.

THE END

To follow another path, turn to page 11.
To read the conclusion, turn to page 101.

"Please," you plead with the old man, "take my sister. She won't take up much room."

The man looks long and hard at you. "Come on, son," he says at last. "You're both getting into this boat."

The big woman and several others voice their disapproval. But the man quiets them and lifts you and your sister into the boat. The boat sinks a little lower into the ocean but not low enough to let in water.

You lean back, Miriam's arms clinging tightly to your neck. Your thoughts are with your father and mother. You pray they are safe as the boat pulls farther away from the sinking *Lusitania*.

33

THE END

To follow another path, turn to page 11.
To read the conclusion, turn to page 101.

You won't take no for an answer. You pull yourself up and reach to get your sister. The old man turns away from you.

"What are you doing?" he cries. He's not talking to you but to the large lady who is standing and holding an oar. Before the man can stop her, she swings the oar at your head. She only delivers a glancing blow, but it's enough to really hurt. You remember Miriam and scoop her out of the water.

The old man is trying to disarm the woman, but other people grab and hold him. You look up and see the woman is about to take another swing at you. You cover Miriam with your body, close your eyes, and brace yourself for another blow. Instead you hear a scream. You open your eyes. The woman has lost her balance and has plunged into the water.

The old man covers you and your shivering sister with his coat. People are calling for him to save the woman in the water. But by now she has disappeared from view.

You watch the *Lusitania* sink. In a few hours you are rescued by a ship called *Flying Fish*. But for now you can't keep your eyes open, and you fall asleep with your arms around your sister.

35

THE END

To follow another path, turn to page 11.
To read the conclusion, turn to page 101.

The suction from the sinking ship could pull lifeboats underwater if they were too close.

"I can't do it," you tell your father. He grabs you with his hands and holds you to his chest.

"We've got to do it, son," he whispers. "It's the only way." Before you can answer, there is a loud crash. *Lusitania* is slipping down into the watery depths. You and your father are falling with it.

THE END

To follow another path, turn to page 11.
To read the conclusion, turn to page 101.

You cling to the piece of driftwood with your father beside you. Soon your hands are so cold you can hardly keep your grip on the driftwood. Your father sees your predicament. A bigger piece of wreckage from the sunken ship floats by, and he hoists you atop it. You lie there gasping for air.

"Rest and be still," he tells you. "A ship or boat will come rescue us."

You wonder how long your father can hold on to the wreckage. There isn't enough room for both of you to be atop it. It seems like hours pass by. Then you hear the sound of a horn in the distance.

"It's a ship!" cries your father, almost slipping under the water with excitement.

Turn the page.

It's a fishing boat, and crewmembers pull you and your father aboard. The boat is already crowded with survivors, all looking as exhausted as the two of you. Soon you are on land in the nearby town of Queenstown, Ireland.

It's late, but together with your father you search for your mother and sister. You find your sister among the survivors, but your mother is missing. You will never see her again. But there is one other passenger you are looking for as well. The next morning, after a good night's sleep, you go into the Cunard office. "Has anyone seen Mr. Vanderbilt?" you ask the man at the desk.

He looks at you sadly and shakes his head. "Sorry, lad," he says. "But we believe Mr. Vanderbilt went down with the ship. Someone said they saw him giving his life jacket to a woman."

Alfred Vanderbilt helped many passengers to safety.

"Thank you, sir," you say, keeping the full story of Mr. Vanderbilt's final sacrifice to yourself.

THE END

To follow another path, turn to page 11.
To read the conclusion, turn to page 101.

A woman reads in the regal bedroom suite aboard the *Lusitania*.

CHAPTER 3

NIGHTMARE HONEYMOON

It's late morning, May 7, 1915, the last day of your honeymoon cruise. Two weeks earlier in New York City, you and Peter were married. Peter is the son of a wealthy New York family. Now you are returning to your homeland, England, on the *Lusitania* to visit your family. Then you will go back to New York and live on the Hudson River in the mansion where Peter grew up.

The voyage across the Atlantic has been wonderful. You have a lovely honeymoon suite. And you have met wonderful people on board. They include actress Rita Jolivet, architect Theodate Pope, and millionaire George Kessler.

Turn the page.

You and Peter have been guests at several parties hosted by Mr. Kessler on board the ship. But your favorite celebrity is the theater producer Charles Frohman, who tells wonderful stories. Today you are meeting Mr. Frohman and Miss Jolivet for your last lunch on the *Lusitania*. By tonight you will be arriving in Liverpool, England.

You and Peter enter the dining salon and find your friends sitting at a table. "Here we are landing today, and I must say I'm deeply disappointed," says Frohman.

"Whatever for?" asks Jolivet. "Well, my dear," he says, lighting a cigar, "I fully expected we would be chased around by a German U-boat. But it hasn't happened."

Suddenly the room shakes. "What's that?" asks Peter.

All around you people are murmuring and getting up from their tables. Frohman looks quite happy. "Something's happened on deck," he says. "Shall we go up and see?"

The four of you follow the other passengers out on deck. The ship's officers tell you that a torpedo has hit the *Lusitania*. "Is the ship going to sink?" asks Frohman.

"I doubt that, sir," says the officer, "but we must follow safety precautions. Women and children should get into the lifeboats."

"I'd rather stay here," says Jolivet. "I'll get all wet and dirty in a lifeboat."

"Exactly," says Frohman. "You stay with me, dear. I'll take care of you."

Peter doesn't agree. "I think you should get into a lifeboat," he tells you.

Turn the page.

Charles Frohman was an American theatrical producer.

You suddenly remember your jewelry in your suite. If the ship does sink, it will be lost forever. "My jewelry!" you cry.

"Do you want me to get it?" Peter asks.

→ To go with Peter to get the jewelry, go to page **45**.

→ To forget the jewelry, turn to page **47**.

→ To send Peter for the jewelry, turn to page **63**.

"Yes, and I'll go with you," you reply. You say good-bye for now to your friends and head downstairs. You pass many passengers rushing in the opposite direction. You wonder if it is a good idea to be doing this when time may be so precious.

You reach your suite and gather up your jewels in a carpetbag. When you get back into the passageway, it is crowded with people. You work your way slowly to the staircase. It is mobbed with passengers trying to get out on deck to see what's happening.

"This will take too long," Peter says. "Maybe we should take the elevator. It won't be so crowded."

➤ *To take the elevator, turn to page 46.*
➤ *To take the stairs, turn to page 48.*

You cram into the elevator with a group of other people. You're packed together like sardines in a can. Someone pushes the button for an upper deck. The elevator smells of sweat and dirt. You cling to your husband as the elevator rises. Suddenly the lights go out, and the elevator comes to an abrupt stop.

"What's happened?" a woman cries.

"The power's gone out," says a man in the front of the elevator. "The ship is listing so much that the lines must have gotten wet and shorted the electricity."

"We're trapped!" cries a woman.

"If we all make noise, maybe someone will hear us and get us out of here," Peter suggests.

→ *Turn to page 65.*

"Forget the jewels," you say. "There isn't time."

"Are you sure?" Peter asks.

"Absolutely," you reply. "But I'm also sure I don't want to be separated from you. Not even for a short time. So we'll forget about the lifeboat for now."

Peter is about to argue, but he sees the firmness in your face and decides against it.

"All right," he sighs. "Let's see if we can find out what's happening to the ship."

"Have fun," says Frohman, puffing on his cigar. "Isn't this exciting?"

Turn to page 50.

The stairs are filled with passengers, but you and Peter finally make your way up to the deck above. People on the port side are lining up to get into a lifeboat. Men are hugging and kissing their wives and children before the women and children climb into the boat.

"You've got to go in a lifeboat," Peter says, and this time he means it.

"I won't leave you," you tell him.

"Look at all the lifeboats," he says with a wave of his hand. "I'll be in a later one. Don't worry."

You don't know whether to believe him. There are a lot of lifeboats, but whether the crew will be able to launch them all in time to get everyone off the ship is another question.

"All right," you say and offer him the carpetbag.

A child is lifted into a lifeboat.

He gently pushes it back to you. "You'd better keep that," Peter says. "Just in case."

Tears well up in your eyes as a sailor helps you into a lifeboat.

Turn to page 52.

You find an officer on deck directing people into a lifeboat. "What chance do we have on the ship?" Peter asks him.

The man shakes his head sadly. "We're taking on water fast. The ship can't last long. I'd get your wife in a lifeboat, sir."

Peter turns to you. "You hear that?" he asks, this time determined to get you into a lifeboat.

The officer pulls the two of you aside. "Listen," he says quietly. "There's extra seats in this boat, and we could use another man to help row. You can join your wife, sir."

A hand falls on your shoulder. You turn and see a woman in a long dress. "I wouldn't get in that boat, ma'am," she says to you.

"But there's room for the both of us," you tell her.

"And why do you think that is?" replies the woman. "People are afraid of what will happen. Half the lifeboats have tipped over before reaching the water, and the people inside fell to their deaths. I'm going for the collapsible boats. They're safer. Follow me, and I'll show you."

Peter is listening to her too. You look at each other. What should you do?

→ To get in the lifeboat, turn to page **53**.

→ To go for the collapsible boats, turn to page **56**.

The lifeboat is filled with crying children and mothers, young women and older children. It swings into the side of the ship as the men lower it. The listing of the ship has put the lifeboat at a dangerously reckless angle.

The carpetbag slips out of your lap and falls overboard just before you reach the ocean's surface. All your jewelry! You must retrieve it before it falls to the bottom of the ocean.

the deck of the *Lusitania*

➤ *Turn to page* **54**.

"Let's go for the lifeboat," you say to Peter. "I trust the crew more than this woman."

"I agree," he says, and you take your places in the lifeboat. When the boat is filled, the crew begins to lower it with ropes.

As the boat is lowered, the listing of the ship causes it to wildly sway back and forth. You see a small girl slide away from her mother and fall against the side of the boat. At any moment the girl could be flung over the side to her death. You could go and grab her, but then you might fall out of the boat too. You have to think fast.

53

→ To try to reach the girl, turn to page **57**.

→ To stay where you are, turn to page **61**.

You dive into the water, but the carpetbag sinks quickly. There's no way you're going to reach it before it disappears into the dark water below. So much for your jewelry.

Before you can get back into the boat, you realize the boat has floated away. You cry out, but the other people on the lifeboat have little sympathy for you. You have let your greed endanger your life and possibly everyone onboard.

But wait. Another lifeboat is coming near! It has room and picks you up. You shiver in your wet clothes and wait to see other lifeboats come from the ship. There are only a few more that reach the water before the *Lusitania* sinks into the sea. You pray that Peter is in one of them.

You have managed to fall asleep in the lifeboat when suddenly you hear people murmuring. A rescue ship has spotted you! When it arrives, you and the others in your lifeboat clamber aboard. Crewmembers take you and the other survivors belowdecks, where they give you mugs of steaming tea and strawberry tarts.

By evening you reach shore and are taken to Queenstown, Ireland. You are given clean clothes and a bed for the night at the Queen's Hotel.

Your every thought is about Peter. Did he get off the ship in time? So many have died, but you don't want to think about that. At first light you leave your room and wander the streets to find your lost husband.

Turn to page 68.

You decide to follow the woman's advice and head for the collapsible boats on deck. A group of passengers are gathered around them, but the boats haven't been moved.

"They're locked on the deck," a bald man tells you and Peter. "Can't budge a one of them. They're perfectly useless."

You turn to your husband. "What are we going to do now?"

Peter looks grim. "Too late for the lifeboat," he says. "It's either stay on board and go down with the ship or jump for it."

56

Either way your chances of survival may be slim, but you must make a choice.

➤ To stay on the ship, turn to page **58**.

➤ To jump and swim for it, turn to page **66**.

You rush to grab the girl. You get your arms around her, but the boat tips. The two of you tumble out into the freezing water.

People are shouting to you from the lifeboat, but you are too busy struggling to keep your head above the waves to hear what they are saying. You have one arm gripped tightly around the little girl's waist while you tread water with the other.

You see Peter throwing a thick rope from the side of the boat. "Grab it!" he cries.

You reach the rope and hold on for dear life.

Turn to page 67.

"I can't do it," you tell Peter. "I'll drown. But you go. At least you have a chance of making it out alive."

Peter stares at you.

"Are you crazy?" he asks. "I'd never leave you. Come on. Let's lie down in one of these collapsible boats. Maybe it'll separate from the ship and float when the ship sinks."

That seems unlikely, but you play along and lie down inside the boat. You are side by side, holding hands. There is a tremendous crack. The *Lusitania* is going down. You grip Peter's hand and close your eyes. You feel the ship sinking. But when you open your eyes a few moments later, you are in for a shock. You're in the collapsible boat, floating on the water! Peter was right. The boat came loose from the deck and stayed on the surface while the great ship sank.

The *Lusitania* made a tremendous cracking sound as it sank.

Suddenly you feel the boat rocking. You look up and see hands gripping the sides of the boat. Other passengers, already in the water, are trying to pull themselves aboard. There is plenty of room in the boat for more people, but they may overturn the boat in the process, sending you all into the water.

Turn the page.

"Stop it!" cries Peter. "You'll capsize us!"

But these people are in a panic and are not listening. They are trying to claw their way into the boat, and it rocks dangerously back and forth.

Peter grabs an oar. He is prepared to strike those clinging to the boat. He feels there is no choice if you are to survive. Do you let him do this or try to stop him?

➤ To let Peter drive the people away from your boat, turn to page **69**.

➤ To stop him from striking them, turn to page **70**.

You decide it's too risky to help the girl.

Just then a man grabs the girl in both arms.

You breathe a sigh of relief as the man hands

the girl back to her weeping mother.

A memorial to the *Lusitania* was created at Queenstown (now Cobh) in Ireland.

Turn the page.

The boat continues to be lowered. It finally hits the water with a loud plop. Peter and the other two men aboard grab oars and start to row as quickly as they can.

"We've got to get far enough away from the ship before she goes down," Peter says. "Otherwise we'll be sucked down with her."

The next two hours pass slowly. The *Lusitania* is long gone, but you are still afloat. A fishing boat picks you up. Finally you arrive late that night in Queenstown, Ireland.

You and Peter sleep in a hotel. The next morning you'll find out who else survived the disaster.

THE END

To follow another path, turn to page 11.
To read the conclusion, turn to page 101.

"Yes, Peter," you reply. "If you wouldn't mind."

"Stay right here," he says. "I'll be back as quickly as I can."

Minutes pass. People are rushing by you from all directions. Where can Peter be? An officer stops and stares at you.

"Madam, you should be getting into a lifeboat," he says.

"I'm waiting for my husband," you explain. "I'll get in the next one."

The officer looks distressed.

"Ma'am, I don't know if there'll be time to launch another lifeboat. I suggest you get into this one leaving now and quickly."

Turn the page.

You begin to protest, but the officer directs two sailors to help you into the lifeboat. The lifeboat is lowered with you and many other women and children in it. Within a few minutes the *Lusitania* crashes into the sea.

Later that night, safe on shore, you search for Peter among the other survivors. There is no sign of him. You sacrificed your husband's life for a handful of jewels. You will live with that guilt for the rest of your life.

64

THE END

To follow another path, turn to page 11.
To read the conclusion, turn to page 101.

Everyone in the elevator raises their voices calling out, "Help! We're stuck in the elevator!" You hear voices above, but no one responds to your cries. You hear heavy footsteps on the deck above. The men and women surrounding you in the darkness are moaning, crying, and praying.

You and Peter hold each other tightly. You are still holding him when the ship sinks with you trapped in the elevator. If only you had taken the stairs!

65

THE END

To follow another path, turn to page 11.
To read the conclusion, turn to page 101.

You're not a great swimmer, but you decide to jump. Peter grips your hand, and you climb atop the railing. You say a quick prayer and jump.

It's not far to the water, but its icy coldness numbs you. You rise to the surface and see Peter a few feet away. He swims alongside you.

"Faster," he says. "We've got to ..."

His words are cut off by a tremendous roar. The *Lusitania* sinks to the ocean floor, and it's pulling you down too. You struggle to stay above the water, but the suction caused by the sinking ship is too strong. Down you sink with your husband by your side, never to emerge again.

THE END

To follow another path, turn to page 11.
To read the conclusion, turn to page 101.

66

Peter and another man pull you in on the rope. You hand the child back to her grateful mother. "What a brave woman I married," Peter says, holding you close.

You try to reply but are so cold that you can barely talk. Peter wraps a blanket around you. Two hours later a rescue ship picks you up and takes you to nearby Queenstown, Ireland. Another boat takes you to Liverpool, England. From there you take a train to London, where your family is anxiously waiting. But your happy ending is short lived. Once in London, the chill you caught turns to pneumonia. Three days later, surrounded by your beloved husband and family, you die, one of the last victims of the sinking of the *Lusitania*.

THE END

To follow another path, turn to page 11.
To read the conclusion, turn to page 101.

Many of the dead were buried together in a large grave in Ireland.

The dead are displayed in three morgues. You look for the body of your husband. You are ready to give up when you bump into a man. It's Peter!

You embrace and weep in his arms. There will be time enough later to tell each other your stories of survival. Now it is enough that you are alive and together.

THE END

To follow another path, turn to page 11.
To read the conclusion, turn to page 101.

68

You don't try stopping Peter. Perhaps this is the only way to stay alive through this disaster.

Peter swings at a man's hands to drive him away from the boat. But the man is faster and manages to grab the oar. He pulls on the oar, and Peter is thrown off balance. He tumbles into the water.

You try to reach for Peter and fall out of the boat as well. You hit your head against someone or something and are knocked unconscious. You sink down into a sleep from which you will never awaken.

THE END

To follow another path, turn to page 11.
To read the conclusion, turn to page 101.

What Peter is doing is murder. You know if you let him hurt anyone, both of you will be haunted by guilt. You grab his hand before he can strike.

"No, Peter, you can't do this," you say.

He looks into your eyes and drops the oar. As the people in the water seize the sides of the boat, the vessel turns over. But you don't panic. You and Peter grab on to the side of the boat along with the others.

With great effort you are able to flip the boat over again. One by one everyone holding on to the boat climbs inside. The oars are gone, and you drift in the water for what seems like hours. Finally a rescue boat picks you up. You and the others arrive late that night in Queenstown, Ireland, where you are put up at a hotel.

Victims are rescued by a fishing boat.

The next morning a grim sight greets you. Bodies retrieved from the water are lined up for identification by friends and relatives who have survived.

You begin to cry for the many hundreds of people who died on the *Lusitania*. You will never forget them as long as you live.

THE END

To follow another path, turn to page 11.
To read the conclusion, turn to page 101.

CHAPTER 4

SAILOR TO THE RESCUE

You are having breakfast in New York City May 1, 1915, with your best friend, Al. It's the last meal you will be eating on land for a week. Today you and Al set sail as crewmembers on the British luxury liner *Lusitania*.

At age 22 you are an experienced sailor. But you've never worked on a passenger ship before. As you drink your coffee, you open the newspaper and a notice catches your eye.

"Maybe we shouldn't go, Al," you say. "Read this."

Turn the page.

"Travellers intending to embark on the Atlantic voyage are reminded that a state of war exists between Germany and her allies and Great Britain and her allies," the ad reads. The notice goes on to say that a war zone exists around the British Isles. "Vessels flying the flag of Great Britain or of any of her allies, are liable to destruction in those waters and that travellers sailing in the war zone on ships of Great Britain or her allies do so at their own risk." The notice is signed by the Imperial German Embassy in Washington, D.C.

Al laughs. "That's just German propaganda," he says. "Anyway, the *Lusitania* is equipped with rings for mounting guns if we run into trouble. And even if the ship is hit by a German submarine, there are enough lifeboats to get every person off safely."

"I guess you're right," you say. "Nothing to worry about."

You finish breakfast and head to the dock where the *Lusitania* is moored. You get on board and take your places as the passengers begin to arrive. Captain William Turner is a seasoned sailor, and you feel safe under his command.

The *Lusitania* sets sail. You enjoy working on a passenger ship, especially one with such wealthy and celebrated passengers.

The morning of May 7 is foggy. You are approaching the coast of Ireland and should arrive in Liverpool early the next morning. By lunchtime the fog has lifted. Shortly after lunch you are on deck when a loud explosion rocks the ship. It is followed by another, louder explosion. You feel the ship beginning to list, a possible sign that it has been hit by a torpedo.

Turn the page.

Passengers hear the ship's alarm sound and begin to panic. You see Al. Together you run to where the lifeboats are stored on the A deck, also known as the boat deck. Other crewmembers join you to get the lifeboats down on the starboard side and load people into them.

Lifeboats line the deck of the ship.

As the ship continues to list to starboard, you see that lowering the lifeboats will not be easy. On the sinking starboard side, they will swing out, away from the ship, and people may fall out of them. But you must try.

Just as you are ready to lower the first boat for passengers to get in, a staff officer appears and tells you to stop.

"We don't need the lifeboats," he says. "The ship is in no danger of sinking."

You've been on a sinking ship once before, and you know this one's in trouble too. But if you disobey a direct order, you may never work on a Cunard ship again.

➤ *To obey the officer's order, turn to page **78**.*
➤ *To continue to lower the lifeboats, turn to page **81**.*

You and the other crewmembers retie the lifeboat. The passengers milling about are relieved, but you're not sure they should be.

Suddenly another sailor runs up and whispers in your ear. "I just got word from the captain that the ship is sinking. He says we may have only 20 minutes before she goes under. Man the lifeboats."

You tell Al what you've just heard. "Maybe we should lower the lifeboats on the port side," Al says. "It's higher than the starboard side, and it should be easier to get the boats safely down into the water."

You're not sure Al is right. There are also collapsible lifeboats on another part of the deck. They are easier to handle and may be a safer bet.

➧ *To go for the port side lifeboats, go to page* **79**.
➧ *To go for the collapsible boats, turn to page* **95**.

You and Al join the other sailors on the port side. You loosen the first lifeboat from its rack. But it quickly becomes clear lowering the lifeboats will be a challenge.

If the starboard side boats swing out from the ship, the problem here is the opposite. Because the ship is higher on the port side, the lifeboats will swing back into the side of the ship, possibly knocking people off the boat.

But there is little time. You must do something. You lower a boat and fill it with women and children. You and Al try to lower it slowly, but the boat swings out and hits the ship's side hard. Several people fall out of the boat and into the water. Then the lifeboat swings back again at the ship and cracks open like an eggshell. The remaining passengers spill into the sea.

Turn the page.

Some passengers thought they saw a U-boat before the *Lusitania* sank.

The other men want to lower another boat. They think they can keep it away from the ship. Can they? You don't want to see others drown.

You see many passengers without life jackets. Maybe you'd be better off spending your time finding life jackets for them. Then you can figure out what to do next to get them off the ship.

➤To lower another lifeboat, turn to page **82**.

➤To look for more life jackets, turn to page **84**.

You're not going to let this officer stop you from saving people from a sinking ship. You continue to lower the lifeboat with the other crewmembers. When the officer tries to stop you, several other men grab him and pin him to the deck. The lifeboat is lowered, and you begin to help women and children into it.

One woman is unusually tall. You look down and see she is wearing men's shoes. This is no woman, but a man in disguise trying to sneak into the first lifeboat. His cowardly attempt makes you ill. What kind of man would resort to this trick? Your first impulse is to haul him off the lifeboat. However, time is short, and maybe it's not worth the trouble.

To ignore him and continue loading boats, turn to **90**.

To get the man off the lifeboat, turn to page **94**.

You will stay with the lifeboats. It's the best way, you decide, to make use of the little time left before the ship goes down. The second boat makes it to the water below loaded with passengers. You, Al, and the other crewmembers give a loud cheer.

Suddenly an officer taps you on the shoulder. "We need a couple of men to get people out of the first-class dining rooms and on deck," he said. "I'm afraid some people aren't taking this situation seriously." You and Al agree to help.

You and Al circulate through the dining rooms, urging people to get their life jackets on and go on deck. Most of them immediately leave, but a few look stunned and are slower to move. You recognize a lone man sitting on the café veranda. He is Harry, a kind, older steward.

"Harry," you say, "time to get on deck. The ship is sinking. There's not much time left."

Harry turns to you with a sad smile. "Do you know I've been on the *Lusitania* since she first sailed across the Atlantic?" he asks.

"Really?" you reply.

"This ship and I are old friends, and I won't leave her now," he says with a sigh.

Poor Harry! He's determined to stay aboard no matter what. Do you leave him to the fate he has chosen? Or do you try to convince him to leave with you?

➤ To leave Harry and go back to the lifeboats, turn to page **88**.

➤ To try to convince Harry to leave, turn to page **96**.

You go to the lounge looking for life jackets and see a crewmember lugging a stack of them. He readily gives you half of them to give to passengers.

You start distributing the jackets on the deck, handing them to anyone who needs one. You help a woman and her daughter into their life jackets, and the grateful mother thanks you. You tell her to wait in line for a lifeboat, hoping this time Al and the others can lower it properly.

A survivor continues to wear his life jacket after being rescued.

Out of life jackets, you try to help an elderly man who is struggling to put his on. He pushes you away. He thinks you want to take his life jacket from him. Can't the fool see you are already wearing a life jacket?

You spot a small girl crying amidst the milling crowd of frightened passengers. "Where's your mother?" you ask her.

"I don't know," she says. "I lost her."

You see another lifeboat is almost ready to be loaded with people. You want to put the girl into it, but she isn't wearing a life jacket. You could give her yours or try to find her another. But there isn't much time.

Turn the page.

You rip off your life jacket and tie it quickly around the little girl. She stares up at you, her eyes wide with surprise. "What will you wear?" she asks.

"Don't worry," you tell her. "I'll find another." But you're not so sure you will.

You lift the girl into the boat and hand her to an older woman. "But what about my mother?" the little girl cries. "We'll find her later, dear," says the kind woman, holding the girl tight.

The boat is filled. "Lower her!" you shout. The men lower the lifeboat, and the little girl waves to you as it descends safely to the sea below.

You and Al fill another lifeboat. You are about to start lowering it when a woman in the boat cries out. "Wait! We can't steer this boat by ourselves. We need someone strong to help us!"

Crewmember J. Roper (right) rescued many people and was hailed as a hero.

"Go on," Al says, nudging you. "Help them out. I'm a better swimmer than you are."

He's right about that, but you don't feel good about leaving your crewmates on a sinking ship. But the women and children need help. There's little time left, and your friends are eager to get another lifeboat off the racks. You've got to decide.

→ To get into the lifeboat, turn to page **90**.

→ To stay on the ship, turn to page **97**.

You can see Harry has made up his mind. It's his choice to stay, and you feel you must accept that. You leave him there at the table, alone and at peace.

On the deck again with Al, you find nothing peaceful. Passengers are running up to you and asking for advice.

"Jump," you say. "It's your only option left."

And that's exactly what you and Al plan to do. The starboard side is the lowest point on the ship, but there are so many people jumping from it that the water around it is clogged with flailing bodies. The port side is a longer jump, but there are fewer people obstructing the water. You opt to jump off the starboard side.

➤ *Turn to page* **98**.

You find a crewmember below deck with life jackets to distribute. You take one, but by the time you get back on the deck, the little girl is gone.

A beautiful woman rushes up to you. You recognize her as the actress Rita Jolivet. "Can you help me, sir?" she gasps. "I can't get this life jacket to fit properly."

You smile and adjust the straps. "Come on," you tell her. "Let's get you into a lifeboat."

You realize that no one in this lifeboat seems to be taking charge, so you get in behind her. You're determined to do all you can to make sure these people are safe. Soon you are rowing for dear life. The *Lusitania* has gone under. After what seems like an eternity, another ship comes into sight. You are saved!

Turn to page **99**.

You climb into the lifeboat. As it hits the water, you grab an oar. You've got to get away from the ship as quickly as possible. If not, your boat will be sucked down to the bottom of the ocean with the sinking ship.

Minutes pass. Suddenly there is a gigantic crash. The great ship's stern disappears under the ocean's surface. "It's gone," a woman says in a hushed whisper.

You shiver from the cold. Your arms ache, but you never stop rowing. Some of the others who had been rowing are lying back, exhausted from their efforts. But two hearty women continue to keep up with you.

Suddenly you hear a weak voice cry out. You look over the side and see a young man clinging to a piece of debris beside the lifeboat. You find the energy to lift him from the water.

People frantically row
to get away from the
sinking ship.

"No! We don't have room for another," one
woman yells. "She's right," says an old man. "Let
him in and the boat will sink for sure."

You don't think he's right, but he may be.
Should you jeopardize the others to try to save
the life of this one man?

→ To leave the man where he is, turn to page **92**.

→ To take the man into the boat, turn to page **93**.

You don't want to give up on the man in the water, but you feel you have little choice. The boat may go under with his added weight. You have to think of the others.

You turn away, ashamed of your actions, and look out to the land. It seems so close, but it's not close enough.

Suddenly you see a boat coming toward you. It is a fishing boat, and it is coming to rescue you! As the boat draws near, you can see the fishermen on board ready to tie up to you.

92

You turn and see the man in the water still struggling. "Get him first!" you cry to the fishermen. And they do. Then it's your turn.

➤ *Turn to page* **99**.

You can't let this man die. You lift him into the boat, and you see the boat sink a little deeper. Water starts to trickle in from the sides. The water will continue to come in until it swamps the boat. Someone needs to get out of the boat—now. You decide it will be you.

You hold on to the side of the boat. Your hands ache from the cold. An hour passes. You know you can't hold on much longer, but if you get back into the boat, you'll probably drown them all.

You let go of the boat. Your last thought before you go under is that you have done the right thing.

THE END

To follow another path, turn to page 11.
To read the conclusion, turn to page 101.

Bodies and debris float on the water after the ship sinks.

You place a hand firmly on the man's shoulder. "I'm sorry, sir, but this boat is for women and children only."

The man's face turns red. He pulls away from you, and you both lose your balance. The two of you tumble overboard, plunging to the water below. *Lusitania* will sink shortly, but you, and the man in women's clothing, will not live to see it.

THE END

To follow another path, turn to page 11.
To read the conclusion, turn to page 101.

94

You find the collapsible boats on the open deck. They can float free if not lowered before the ship sinks. They seem like a good alternative to the lifeboats.

You grab one collapsible boat, but it is bolted to the deck. Too late you learn that Captain Turner had this done earlier so the boats wouldn't slide along the deck.

As you decide what to do next, the ship begins to sink. One of the ship's huge funnels collapses and comes crashing down on you. It sweeps you off the deck, and you tumble down into the freezing water. The impact of the funnel blow kills you before you hit the water. It is a quicker death than drowning.

THE END

To follow another path, turn to page 11.
To read the conclusion, turn to page 101.

You can't let Harry stay here and face certain death. You sit down, and he looks at you in surprise. You try to find the words that will convince him to leave the ship with you.

"Listen, Harry," you begin. "You can't just give up like this. Not when there's still a chance you can make it out alive."

Harry opens his mouth to reply, but before he can get a word out, the ceiling collapses. It must have been crushed by chairs and equipment on the deck above as the ship continued to list.

The roof and the falling objects strike both you and Harry, killing you instantly. By staying with Harry, you have shared his fate.

THE END

To follow another path, turn to page 11.
To read the conclusion, turn to page 101.

"I'm not leaving this ship," you tell Al. "Not yet."

"Don't be stupid," Al growls back. "Those people need you."

"If you think that, then get into the boat yourself," you say.

Al realizes one of you must act and act quickly. He climbs into the lifeboat.

"You get in the next one," he says to you as the lifeboat is lowered.

But there will be no next one. Only minutes after Al's lifeboat is lowered, there is a tremendous crash. As you go down with the ship, you think of your best friend who made it out alive. That last thought is a comforting one.

THE END

To follow another path, turn to page 11.
To read the conclusion, turn to page 101.

Al is waiting at the starboard side, ready to jump. You join him, and the two of you dive off the ship.

You are careful to avoid falling into the water on someone else. But other people jumping after you aren't as careful. A large woman lands atop you, pushing you under. You rise only to have another person strike you. You are knocked half unconscious and sink down. You rise and try to swim away from the ship, but struggling passengers are blocking the way.

You see a deck chair several yards away and try to swim for it. But you never get that far. Your last thought as you go under for the last time is the hope that Al has had better luck.

THE END

To follow another path, turn to page 11.
To read the conclusion, turn to page 101.

You climb onto the rescue ship, a fishing boat. A few hours later, the boat docks in Queenstown, Ireland. After a good night's sleep, you head to the temporary office the Cunard Line has set up in the town. There is a list of those who have not yet been found. You look for Al's name.

"Looking for someone?" a familiar voice says behind you. It's Al! "You were right from the start," he says. "We never should have shipped out on the *Lusitania*. Not after seeing that notice in the newspaper. Those Germans meant every word!"

They did, but you're not sorry you were aboard *Lusitania* on its last voyage. You saved many passengers. You and Al are a part of history.

THE END

To follow another path, turn to page 11.
To read the conclusion, turn to page 101.

99

Anti-German riots broke out in London, England, after the sinking of the *Lusitania*.

CHAPTER 5

REMEMBER THE *LUSITANIA*

The sinking of the *Lusitania* remains one of the greatest tragedies at sea in modern times. Of the 1,959 passengers and crew aboard the passenger ship, only 761 survived. Among the 128 Americans who perished were several famous people, including millionaire Alfred Vanderbilt, showman Charles Frohman, and author Elbert Hubbard.

The world's reaction was one of shock and anger at the Germans. A British newspaper's headline called the sinking "The Hun's Most Ghastly Crime." Another called Germany "the renegade among the nations." Anti-German riots and looting of German-owned businesses took place in several British cities.

In the United States anti-German feelings also ran high. President Woodrow Wilson wept upon hearing of the *Lusitania* tragedy. He demanded an apology, financial compensation to the victims and survivors' families, and a promise to abandon "unannounced submarine warfare" on merchant and passenger ships. The American public wanted him to go further and were in a mood for war.

The German government considered the sinking a great success. The U-boat commander, Captain Walter Schwieger, was declared a national hero, and German children were given the day off from school. But as weeks passed, the German government realized it did not want to make the Americans angry enough to enter the war on the Allied side.

The German government sent a note to Wilson expressing its "deepest regrets at the loss of American lives." But no formal apology was made. Instead, the Germans blamed the British for ignoring their threats and for forcing their hand with their blockade.

While Wilson wanted to stay out of the war, he insisted on a German apology and an end to the sub attacks. Secretary of State William Jennings Bryan called for moderation in talks with Germany, but public opinion went against him. Bryan resigned June 8 from the president's Cabinet.

The Germans eventually agreed to end the unrestricted sub attacks on passenger liners. But they dragged their feet on reparations and an apology. Discussions continued, however, and tensions lessened between Germany and the U.S.

Then on February 1, 1917, Germany resumed the sub attacks. Soon after, Wilson cut diplomatic relations with Germany. On April 6 the United States declared war on Germany. The first wave of American soldiers landed in France on June 25.

U.S. support helped lead the Allies to victory over Germany and Austria-Hungary. A year and a half after the U.S. entered the war, Germany signed an armistice. Signed November 11, 1918, the armistice stopped the fighting on the Western Front. Germany signed a peace treaty June 28, 1919, which officially ended World War I.

The sinking of the *Lusitania* played a major role in bringing the United States into the war. But was the passenger ship a warship, as the Germans claimed? Historians have proven that the ship did carry arms from the United States, including 4.2 million rounds of rifle ammunition.

But a claim that the second explosion that sank the ship was the torpedo striking explosives in the hold is still in doubt. Some experts believe the torpedo hit one of the ship's boilers, and that caused the explosion. When oceanographer Robert Ballard explored the ship's wreck in 1993, however, he found the boilers intact.

There have even been claims that the British Admiralty deliberately allowed the *Lusitania* to be exposed to a German sub attack in order to get the United States to join its side in the war. No historical evidence has been found to prove such charges. But the complete truth of the *Lusitania*'s sinking may never be known.

TIMELINE

September 7, 1907—*Lusitania* leaves Liverpool, England, on its maiden voyage; it arrives in New York on September 13.

June 28, 1914—Archduke Franz Ferdinand, heir to the throne of Austria-Hungary, is assassinated, which leads that country to declare war on Serbia.

August 1 and 3, 1914—Germany, ally of Austria-Hungary, declares war on Russia and then France.

August 4, 1914—Germany invades Belgium; Great Britain declares war on Germany.

February 4, 1915—Germany declares a war zone around Great Britain that it will patrol with its submarines.

May 1, 1915—*Lusitania* sets sail from New York bound for Liverpool, England.

May 7, 1915—A German U-boat fires on the *Lusitania* at 2:10 p.m., and the ship sinks within 20 minutes; 1,198 people die.

May 13, 1915—Great Britain, the United States, and other nations condemn the Germans for the sinking of the *Lusitania*.

June 1915—Germany suspends unrestricted submarine attacks on passenger liners in the war zone.

February 1, 1917—The Germans resume unrestricted submarine warfare.

April 6, 1917—The United States declares war on Germany and enters World War I.

June 25, 1917—The first U.S. troops land in France to join the fighting.

November 11, 1918—Germany signs an armistice, ending fighting on the Western Front.

June 28, 1919—Germany signs a peace treaty, officially ending World War I.

OTHER PATHS TO EXPLORE

In this book you've seen how the events surrounding the sinking of the *Lusitania* look different from several points of view. Perspectives on history are as varied as the people who lived it. Seeing history from many points of view is an important part of understanding it.

Here are ideas for other points of view to explore:

+ We now know that the *Lusitania* was carrying weapons. Why would the ship be carrying arms and ammunition? (Common Core: Key Ideas and Details)

+ Passengers had to make choices once it was clear the *Lusitania* was going to sink. What would happen if they chose to go in a lifeboat? What would happen if they decided to stay aboard the ship? (Common Core: Craft and Structure)

+ The sinking of the *Lusitania* helped draw the United States into the war. Why do you think this one event helped tip the scales when other events had not had that effect? (Common Core: Integration of Knowledge and Ideas)

READ MORE

Freedman, Russell. *The War To End All Wars: World War I.* Boston: Clarion Books, 2010.

Hunter, Nick. *The Home Fronts in World War I.* Chicago: Capstone Heinemann Library, 2014.

Kent, Zachery. *World War I: From the Lusitania to Versailles.* Berkeley Heights, N.J.: Enslow Publishers, 2011.

INTERNET SITES

Use FactHound to find Internet sites related to this book. All of the sites on FactHound have been researched by our staff.

Here's all you do:
Visit *www.facthound.com*
Type in this code: 9781476541860

GLOSSARY

armistice (ARM-iss-tiss)—formal agreement to end the fighting during a war

blockade (blok-AYD)—a closing off of an area to keep people or supplies from going in or out

list (LIST)—to lean to one side

moored (MOORED)—secured by cables, ropes, or anchors

port (PORT)—the left side of a ship looking forward

propaganda (praw-puh-GAN-duh)—information spread to try to influence the thinking of people; often not completely true or fair

prow (PROU)—the front part of a ship

reparations (reh-puh-RAY-shuns)—payments made to make amends for wrongdoing

starboard (STAR-burd)—the right side of a ship looking forward

steward (STOO-urd)—the ship's officer who is in charge of food and meals; a steward is also an attendant on a ship

veranda (vuh-RAN-duh)—a large, open porch with a roof

BIBLIOGRAPHY

Halliday, E.M. "Who Sank the Lusitania?" *American Heritage,* December 1975, pp. 33-35, 96.

Handlin, Oscar. "A Liner, A U-Boat ... and History." *American Heritage,* June 1955, pp. 40-45, 105.

Lewis, Jon E., ed. *The Permanent Book of The 20th Century: Eye-Witness Accounts of the Moments that Shaped Our Century.* New York: Carroll & Graf, 1994.

Massie, Robert K. *Castles of Steel: Britain, Germany and the Winning of the Great War at Sea.* New York: Random House, 2003.

Preston, Diana. *Lusitania: An Epic Tragedy.* New York: Walker & Company, 2002.

Index